CREATURES ALL AROUND US

Eight Legs

by D. M. Souza

Carolrhoda Books, Inc./Minneapolis

Many of the photos in this book show the spiders larger than life size. The degree of magnification varies.

Library of Congress Cataloging-in-Publication Data

Souza, D. M. (Dorothy M.)
  Eight legs / by D. M. Souza.
    p.   cm.
  Summary: Describes the physical characteristics, behavior, and life cycles of various spiders and other arachnids, including the crab spider, wolf spider, and whipscorpion.
    1. Spiders—Juvenile literature. 2. Arachnida—Juvenile literature. [1. Spiders. 2. Arachnids.] I. Title. II. Title: 8 legs.
QL452.2.S68 1991
595.4'4—dc20   90-38293
                                   CIP
                                    AC

Manufactured in the United States of America

2 3 4 5 6 7 8 9 10 00 99 98 97 96 95 94 93 92

Not all spiders spin webs. This Argiope *is one that does.*

Silk Makers

You and a friend are sitting on the floor playing a game. Suddenly, a tiny, eight-legged creature drops on an invisible thread and dangles between you. It twists and turns, falls to the floor, and scurries under a chair.

Outside, another eight-legged creature races across the lawn toward a bee that is sipping nectar from a dandelion. The creature jumps up and bites the bee on the neck. Then it quickly uses its legs to tie up the bee with thin, silk cords.

1

You guessed it. Both of these creatures are spiders. They can be found everywhere—inside homes and other buildings or outside in gardens, parks, or forests. They live in deserts and jungles, on the highest mountains, and even in the icy Arctic. Some have been seen drifting on silken threads far out at sea or floating hundreds of feet in the air.

There are more than 40,000 known types of spiders, and probably many more waiting to be discovered. Spiders belong to a class of animals called **arachnids** (uh-RAK-nids). This class includes not only spiders but also mites, ticks, scorpions, and harvestmen. Unlike insects, which have three pairs of legs, arachnids have four. They have no antennae or wings.

Spiders' bodies are divided into two parts—a front section called a **cephalothorax** (seh-phuh-luh-THOR-aks), and a back section called an **abdomen** (AB-doh-men). Attached to the cephalothorax are eight legs, each ending in two or three claws, and two leglike structures called **palps**.

4

Spiders use the hairs, or setae, on their legs to help them sense what's around them.

Most spiders have eight eyes on their heads, but some have only six, four, or two. Cave-dwelling spiders have none. While some spiders are able to see quite well, many have poor eyesight. They rely on fine hairs, or **setae** (SEE-tee), on their legs and palps to help them hear, feel, and even smell.

Because they cannot chew or swallow anything solid, spiders must turn every meal into a liquid. Their jaws, or **chelicerae** (kuh-LIS-uh-ree), hold captured insects or spiders while sharp fangs inject a poisonous liquid called **venom** (VEH-nuhm). Other liquids turn the victim's soft body parts into a soup that is then pumped into the spider's stomach by powerful muscles.

This wolf spider is holding its victim steady with its powerful jaws, or chelicerae.

On the underside of the spider's abdomen are two openings called **spiracles** (SPIH-ruh-kuhlz) that help it breathe. Near the end of the abdomen are openings called **spinnerets** (SPIN-uh-rehts). With its feet the spider draws out liquid silk from its spinnerets. As soon as air touches the liquid, it turns into a solid thread. These silk threads can be as thin as a millionth of an inch wide, but if twisted together, they can become as strong as steel.

The bodies of young spiders, like those of some insects, are covered with soft, stretchy **cuticles** (KYOO-tih-kuhlz). When the cuticles become too small, they are shed. This process is called **molting**. Before molting, a spider may stop eating and remain inactive for days or even weeks. Pressure from inside the cuticle finally makes it split open, and the spider wiggles out, leaving an empty, eight-legged case behind. Sometimes, if a spider's leg is lost in the struggle to get out of the cuticle, a new one grows in its place. Molting takes anywhere from a half hour to two hours, and during this time, the spider is helpless.

This picture shows a huntsman spider that has just molted, with its shed skin above it.

If you have ever done any spider watching, you know how talented these creatures can be. Some build giant, delicate webs, while others make clever underground traps and tunnels. Some stalk **prey** (insects or other spiders to feed on), skate across the water, or swing through the air hanging by a claw. On the next pages, we'll take a closer look at a few spiders and other arachnids in action.

A crab spider captures its insect prey.

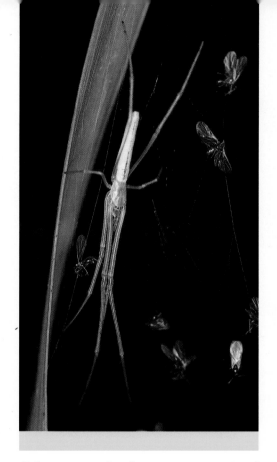

A long-jawed orb weaver in its web, where it has trapped several flies.

Orb Weavers

The word *spider* probably makes you think of a dark, leggy creature hanging upside down in the middle of a gauzy web. But not all spiders spin webs. Only about half the known varieties in the world are able to do so.

Those that do spin webs could not survive without them. They depend on them for trapping prey, hiding from their enemies, and meeting mates.

Web weavers come in all sizes and shapes. Many are shy and, if frightened, will run and hide close by. Most wait in their webs night and day for an insect to come into their traps.

Some spiders build their webs at night and take them down the next morning by eating them. Some leave them in place for weeks or even months. If no insects come along, they build their webs elsewhere.

In and around your home you may find oddly shaped webs in corners of closets, on windowsills, outside on the grass, in shrubs, and on trees. Some look like sheets, pieces of pie, even hammocks. One of the most beautiful webs is built by orb weaver spiders. It is shaped like a wheel and takes only an hour to make. There are many different types of orb weavers, but they all build lovely webs.

First the orb weaver sits on top of a flower, branch, or garden fence. It drops from this perch on a thread of silk called a **dragline**. Next the spider lands on something solid, fastens the end of the line here, and begins its work.

It moves quickly—kicking, running, and spinning out silken threads until the web looks like a wheel with spokes coming out from the center. When the web is almost finished, the spider spins a sticky kind of silk on the outer edges. Insects that land here get stuck, but the orb weaver does not. A special oil on its claws lets it move freely around the web.

Left: *Orb weaver spiders spin beautiful wheel-shaped webs.*

Right: *An orb weaver hangs from a dragline while it spins its web.*

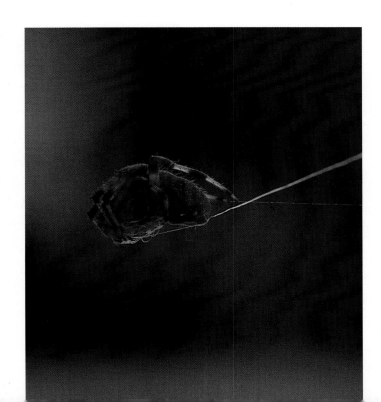

This orb weaver is attacking a damselfly that has landed on the spider's web.

Most of the time, the orb weaver sits in the center of its web. Sometimes it hides under a nearby leaf or in a crack in a fence post and holds on to a thread that is attached to the center of the web. This is its message line. When an insect lands on the web, the line vibrates, and the spider rushes forward. It grabs the insect, wraps it in silk, and pierces it with its fangs. Then the spider either begins feasting or takes the insect meal to a safe place and saves it for a late night snack.

14

When orb weavers mate, they leave their webs to lay eggs on a nearby plant or twig. A female may lay from three to eight hundred eggs, depending upon her size. She covers them with several layers of silk and fastens them in place with special sticky silk.

After the young, or **spiderlings**, are born, they molt several times. Some spiderlings molt only a few times, others as many as 10 times.

Dozens of orb weaver spiderlings are hatching in their nest on a branch.

15

Soon after hatching, spiderlings move away from their nesting places. They scramble to the tips of thin blades of grass or the tops of flowers, and wait.

When a slight breeze blows, each spiderling stretches as tall as it can, lets out a thin line of silk from its spinnerets, and floats upward. This is called **ballooning**. Soon hundreds of strands of silk are drifting overhead and sparkling in the sunlight.

Some spiderlings land only a short distance away, but others are carried far. As soon as they land, all begin putting their silk factories to work weaving unique webs.

Most orb weaver spiderlings move away from the nest after hatching.

16

Jumping spiders such as this one see quite well with their large eyes.

Hunters and Fishers

Bold, strong, and swift are words that describe those spiders that spend their time hunting and fishing instead of weaving traps. They run along the ground, over lakes and ponds, and up and down plants searching for prey. Most have sharp teeth that they use to bite and crush their victims.

Jumping spiders are big-eyed hunters that see quite well. Many are small and antlike. Some are brightly colored and are frequently seen in the sunlight, where they like to hunt.

When a jumping spider spots an insect in the distance, it attaches a silk line to some nearby object, then creeps forward and pounces like a cat. Some of these spiders are able to jump 40 or more times their own body length. If the jumper misses its victim, it uses the silk line to go back to its nest, and later to return and try again.

At night these spiders hide in silk nests under stones or bark, or in crevices or plants. Females lay their eggs here and may also use these nests as shelters on cold days.

Jumping spiders are excellent hunters. This jumping spider has captured a deer fly.

If you look carefully, you'll see the crab spider hiding on this flower.

Crab spiders are hunters that hold their legs like a crab's and can move backward and sideways as well as forward. They hunt day or night, and with their flat bodies they are able to hide in narrow places under bark or stones. Some lie in wait in flower heads and attack insects that come for pollen. Many are the same color as the flowers they hide in and cannot easily be seen.

19

Perhaps the most frequently spotted of the big-eyed hunters are the wolf spiders. They move around day or night and run and chase insects in gardens or parks.

They vary in length from ¼ inch to 1½ inches or more. On the lower part of each wolf spider's face is a row of four small eyes that see both sideways and frontward. Above these are two very large eyes that also see forward. On top of the wolf spider's head are two more large eyes that see upward. Very little movement escapes them.

With its eight eyes, this wolf spider can see sideways, forward, and upward.

20

This female wolf spider is carrying her egg sac with her.

The female wolf spider lays her eggs in a round white sac that is almost as big as she is. She attaches the sac to her spinnerets, drags it around wherever she goes, and defends it with her life. When her young are almost ready to hatch, she bites into a seam in the sac, and hundreds of spiderlings tumble out. Within a few hours, all of them climb onto her back and begin riding piggyback, sometimes two and three deep.

For almost a week, while their mother hunts, runs, fights, and feasts, these spiderlings cling to her and to each other. If one falls off, it must rush to get back on, for its mother will not stop to give it a lift. When they are ready to molt, the spiderlings crawl down from their mother's back and begin lives of their own.

Wolf spiderlings ride on their mother's back for about a week after they hatch.

A female nursery-web spider stands guard over her young in the special nest that she has made for them.

Female nursery-web spiders, which are a type of fishing spider, also carry their egg sacs around with them, but they carry them in their jaws instead of on their abdomens.

Before the young are ready to hatch, the females tie leaves together with silk threads; then hang their egg sacs in the middle of this envelope. The mothers stand guard nearby, and after about a week, the young hatch and leave home.

Many nursery-web spiders live in moist places and, because they are lightweight, can easily run across the surface of a pond or lake. They are also able to dive underwater to search for prey.

Other fisher spiders hide along the banks of rivers and streams and hunt water insects and tadpoles. They too can run over the surface of the water and dive into it. A few even float around on leaves and fish from them.

There are many other hunters and fishers with clever ways of capturing prey. While they have not given up their talent for making silk, none use it in quite the same way as their web-weaving relatives.

The markings on its abdomen tell you that this spider is a black widow.

Dangerous Widow

Hidden in a dark corner of the garage, attic, or basement is a web with threads that zigzag and crisscross each other. These threads are about one hundred times finer than a single hair on your head and are dark and strong. Hanging upside down in the middle of this silk maze is a jet black spider with bright red or yellow markings in the shape of an hourglass on its underside. This creature is a female black widow spider, so called because, if she is hungry enough, she will eat her own mate.

If you frighten her, she will run and hide in a crack or curl up her legs and play dead. However, if you threaten her or her eggs, she may bite and inject a venom that, drop for drop, is more powerful than a rattlesnake's.

Her mate is smaller than she is but has longer legs. He does not stay anywhere for long but wanders from place to place. While the female's venom sac grows larger and more poisonous with age, the male's becomes smaller and weaker. He rarely bites, but if he does, his bite has little effect.

If a female black widow is threatened, she may bite and inject a powerful poison into her victim.

The female black widow has a big appetite and will eat flies, sowbugs, grasshoppers, butterflies, moths, crickets, or any insect that strays onto her web. At the end of her fourth leg are tiny combs of setae that she uses to draw out sticky silk from her spinnerets. She uses this silk to wrap captured prey like a mummy. Once her victim is helpless, she bites it with her fangs and begins her meal.

When ready to lay her eggs, the female black widow makes an egg sac of silk and attaches it to her web. She hangs above it with her head and forelegs pointing upward and releases round, butter-colored eggs into the sac. Some black widows lay 25 eggs, others as many as 1,000. When the last egg falls, the spider seals the opening of the sac and covers it with more silk until it is about the size of a marble. Then she anchors it in place with more thread.

A female black widow sits with her egg sac in her web.

Black widow spiderlings are just beginning to hatch through a hole in their egg sac.

For days or weeks the black widow guards her sac. She may move it into the sun on cold days and if necessary will use her fangs to protect it from attackers.

When the time comes for hatching, the spiderlings bite holes in the egg sac and squeeze through the openings. As soon as air touches them, their soft bodies harden, and they begin moving around the web.

Some draw out a strand of silk from their spinnerets and float away on the first breeze that blows. Others scamper off the web and hide in clumps of grass, piles of wood, or other dark places, where they begin building webs of their own. At first these webs are tiny, but as the spiderlings grow, so do their webs. A few may eventually reach over 3 feet wide.

It takes two to four months for spiderlings to become adults. While many are eaten by birds, insects, or other spiders, some black widows live for over a year.

Black widows have been found around the world, both indoors and out. They have been discovered hiding under furniture, behind books on library shelves, in boxes in garages, and in clumps of grass. If you spot a web weaver with telltale red or yellow markings under its abdomen, study it from a distance. This is one shy-looking spider that can be dangerous!

It takes two to four months for black widow spiderlings to become adults.

A harvestman, or daddy longlegs, perches on a leaf.

Other Arachnids

Spiders are not the only eight-legged creatures you may see inside or outside your house. There are other arachnids that are both curious and interesting.

You've probably spotted harvestmen crowded together on plants, on the trunks of trees, or perhaps in dark corners of your house. Harvestmen's bodies are in one oval piece, and two eyes sit on the tops of their heads. Harvestmen have extremely long legs and are often called daddy longlegs.

A clump of harvestmen crowd together on a tree trunk.

Male harvestmen are smaller than females but have longer legs. Females lay their eggs in the ground in the fall, and their young hatch the next spring. All harvestmen feed on insects—both living and dead—or on the juices of plants.

The telson of the scorpion has a stinger that can deliver a painful sting.

Scorpions have been around for almost 400 million years. They do not look much like spiders. Some are 6 inches long or more, and their palps resemble the claws of a lobster. Their tails, or telsons, end in stingers filled with poison. While scorpion venom causes a painful, burning sensation in humans, usually it is not life-threatening.

The young of scorpions are not hatched from eggs but are born alive. They crawl onto their mothers' backs and stay there until after their first molt. Then they fall off and hide under fallen trees or stones. Some dig shallow tunnels in the earth and burrow during the day. At night they come out to hunt for insects and spiders.

The young of scorpions climb onto their mother's back after they are born.

Whipscorpions have no stingers but have large, grasping palps armed with sharp spines. These help them crush prey. Some have long front legs they use as whips, while others lash out with their tails.

Whipscorpions live in dark, sheltered places. Some burrow into sand and debris and come out at night to hunt insects. They run away quickly when frightened and are harmless to humans.

Whipscorpions (also called vinegarones) such as this one can crush prey with their palps.

This velvet mite likes to eat insect eggs. Other mites, including ticks, may feed on humans.

There are other such eight-legged creatures with strange names and habits. Many are so small we rarely see them. All of them, together with spiders, go quietly about their work of hunting prey and making more of their kind in the hidden world around us.

Scientists who study animals group them together according to their similarities and differences. Animals that have certain features in common are placed in the same **order**. All spiders belong to the order Araneae. Scientists break down orders into smaller groups called families. Some of the families of spiders discussed in this book, along with some of their arachnid relatives, are described below.

ORDER	FAMILY	EXAMPLES	TYPE OF NEST
Araneae	Lycosidae	wolf spiders	some live in burrows, others under stones
	Pisauridae	nursery-web spiders	female builds a special web for her young; adults travel through woods and fields as they hunt
	Thomisidae	crab spiders	none—most wander over flowers and other plants
	Araneidae	orb weavers	round webs, usually on flowers or tree branches
Acari		mites, ticks	on animals, in grass and forests
Opiliones		harvestmen (daddy-long-legs)	on plants and trees
Scorpiones		scorpions	under stones, bark, debris
Uropygi		whipscorpions	under sand, debris

Glossary

abdomen: the back section of a spider's body

arachnids: members of a group of animals having eight legs and no antennae

ballooning: a way of moving in which spiders float through the air on silk threads

cephalothorax: the front section of a spider's body

chelicerae: structures on a spider's cephalothorax that are used to hold captured prey

cuticles: the outer covering of a spider's body

dragline: a silk line that spiders attach to objects as they move from one place to another

molting: shedding a cuticle

palps: leglike structures on a spider's cephalothorax

prey: animals that are killed and eaten by other animals

setae: bristles on a spider's legs that help it sense things around it

spiderlings: baby spiders

spinnerets: openings on a spider's abdomen through which liquid silk leaves the body

spiracles: breathing holes on the underside of a spider's body

venom: a poisonous liquid

Index

The photographs are reproduced through the courtesy of: pp. 3, 11, © George
Rhodes; pp. 5, 9, 11, 21, 23, 25, 27, © John Serrao; p. 6, © Mary Stibritz; pp. 7, 17,
20, 22, 26, 29, 30, 31, 33, 34, 35, 36, 37, © Robert and Linda Mitchell; pp. 10, 12, 19,
Donald L. Rubbelke; pp. 13, 14, 16, 32, © Frank Stibritz; p. 18, front cover (inset),
Dwight R. Kuhn; front cover (background), back cover, © Gerry Lemmo.